TELL ME WHY, TELL ME HOW

WHY DOES THE SUN SET?

TERRY ALLAN HICKS

Marshall Cavendish
Benchmark
New York

Marshall Cavendish Benchmark
99 White Plains Rd.
Tarrytown, NY 10591-5502
www.marshallcavendish.us

Library of Congress Cataloging-in-Publication Data

Hicks, Terry Allan.
Why does the sun set? / by Terry Allan Hicks.
p. cm. — (Tell me why, tell me how)
Summary: "Provides comprehensive information on the process of how and why
the sun sets"—Provided by publisher.
ISBN 978-0-7614-3993-6
1. Sun—Juvenile literature. 2. Earth—Rotation—Juvenile literature. I.
Title.
QB521.5.H53 2010
523.7'3—dc22

2008049027

Photo research by Candlepants Incorporated

Cover Photo: Shutterstock

The photographs in this book are used by permission and through the courtesy of:
Shutterstock: 1, 13. *Getty Images*: Keren Su, 4; Jim Ballard, 6; Manan Vatsyayana/AFP, 7; Henry Georgi , 14;
NASA-JPL-Caltech - Voyager / digital version by Science Faction, 20. *Alamy Images*: Pictorial Press Ltd, 5;
Friedrich Saurer, 8; Trip, 11; Stephen Finn, 22; Betty LaRue, 16. *Terry Allan Hicks*: 15. *Sciencefaction.net*: William
Radcliffe, 10. *Photo Researchers Inc.*: BSIP, 12; Mark Garlick, 17; Fred Burrell, 24; Karsten Schneider, 18.
AnimalsAnimals/Earth Scenes: Khalid Ghani, 21. *Corbis*: Tony Craddock/zefa, 23.

Editor: Joy Bean
Publisher: Michelle Bisson
Art Director: Anahid Hamparian
Series Designer: Alex Ferrari

Printed in Malaysia

1 3 5 6 4 2

CONTENTS

Watching the Sun set at night can be peaceful and relaxing.

The Star of the Show

Every evening, millions of people all over the world take a few minutes out of their busy lives to watch the **Sun** set. For a short time, the setting Sun seems to transform the entire world. It fills the sky with reds, oranges, yellows, and many other dazzling colors. Then darkness falls, and another day comes to an end. This beauty is why sunsets are a favorite subject of painters and photographers.

When the sun sets, it transforms the sky into a show of beautiful colors.

On a clear night, look up at the sky and you will see countless stars in the sky.

But what is really happening when the Sun sets? To answer that question, we need to know more about the star of this light show—the Sun.

The Sun is really a **star**, which is a huge, spinning ball of flaming gas. The Sun makes huge amounts of **energy**, which reaches Earth as **light**. The Sun is not the only star in the sky. You only need to look up on a cloudless night to see that there are almost too many stars to count. Some **astronomers** think there are 70 sextillion—that is the number 7, followed by 22 zeros—stars in the known **universe**.

The Sun is not the biggest star in the sky, and it is not the brightest, either. The largest known star, VY Canis Majoris, is more than two thousand times the size of the Sun. The brightest star, the Pistol Star, may give off five to six million

The safest way to view the Sun is to use the projection method. Point a telescope (or a pair of binoculars with one lens covered) at the Sun, without looking through the eyepiece. Then place a sheet of white paper a short distance from the eyepiece. It will take some time to find the right position, but when you do, an image of the sun will be projected on the paper. It is extremely important not to look through the eyepiece, or to put your hand behind the eyepiece, even for a few seconds. The sun's light can cause severe eye damage and can burn your skin very badly.

times as much light as the Sun. It produces more energy in a minute than the Sun does in an entire year. Even though these stars are the biggest and the brightest we know of in the sky, they are not visible from Earth without a telescope.

Our sun might not be the brightest in the universe, but it is far from dim! You must never look directly at the Sun—even if you are wearing sunglasses—because the Sun's light can permanently damage your eyes.

The Sun is the most important star for living things on Earth because it is the star closest to us. The Sun is about 93

There are eight planets in our Solar System. Earth is the third closest to the Sun.

million miles (150 million kilometers) away from Earth. That seems like a huge distance—and it is, except when compared with how far away other bodies in space are.

The distances in space are so great that scientists created a special unit of measurement for them: the **light-year**. This unit equals how far light travels in one year—about 5.9 trillion miles (9.5 trillion km). The Sun's light takes about eight light-minutes to travel the distance to Earth. The light from the next-closest star, Alpha Centauri, takes 4.3 light years to reach us. Some recently discovered stars are more than a billion light-years away.

The Sun is the biggest and most powerful object in our **Solar System**. The Sun is so big that about one million **planets** the size of Earth could fit inside it. The Sun's power is always at work. It affects Earth and all the other bodies in the Solar System in many ways.

The Sun is by far the largest of all the
bodies in the Solar System, and it has
the most gravity.

A Planet on the Move

The most powerful influence on Earth is **gravity**. This is an invisible force that causes objects to be attracted to one another. All bodies in space—including stars, planets, and **moons**— attract other bodies. The Sun has the strongest gravitational pull of any body in the Solar System because it has the greatest **mass**.

Earth and the other planets are always trying, and failing, to escape from the Sun's gravitational attraction. The result is that they travel in space, trapped in a path around the Sun called an **orbit**. The size of a planet's orbit depends partly on how far away from the Sun it is. It takes one year—about 365 days—for Earth to orbit the Sun.

Earth's gravity holds its moon (shown here) in orbit.

Earth is moving in other ways, too. It is constantly **rotating**, or spinning on its **axis**. This is an invisible line that runs down the center of the planet from the North Pole to the South Pole. All of the planets in the Solar System rotate. The Sun and the Moon rotate, too. Earth rotates in a counter-clockwise direction. It takes Earth one day—about twenty-four hours—to turn around completely.

All the planets in our Solar System, and billions of other objects, orbit the Sun.

Only one side of Earth faces the Sun at any time, so one side is always lit and the other is always dark. When it is daytime in New York City, for example, it is nighttime in Tokyo—and vice versa. And there is always a point, somewhere in the world, where the daytime and nighttime sides of the planet meet. This is where the Sun is "setting." The Sun seems to be moving lower in the sky, taking its light away. In reality, the Sun is not going down. Instead, Earth is rotating on its axis. Meanwhile, on the other side of Earth, someone else is watching the Sun rise.

The Sun seems to drop lower in the sky as the day comes to an end. But it is the Earth that is moving, not the Sun.

13

The Sun sets later in the day in the
summertime than it does during the winter.
This gives you more time to play outside.

☀ What Is Your ☀ Angle?

Have you ever noticed that sunset does not always come at the same time of day? The exact time of the sunset changes throughout the year. When you are on summer vacation, the Sun might not go down until bedtime. But in the winter, the Sun might already have set before you sit down to eat your dinner.

The reason the amount of light in a day changes is that Earth's axis—that invisible line down the center of the planet— is actually at an angle. This angle, called the **axial tilt**, does not change as Earth orbits the Sun. However, the distance

The Sun sets so early in the wintertime that you may need to turn on a light to do your homework.

15

between any point on Earth's surface and the Sun does change. This means that the Sun's energy travels different distances to reach that point at different times. This makes the period of daylight longer or shorter.

On June 21 or 22 every year, Earth passes through a point in its orbit where the **Northern Hemisphere**—the top half of the planet—is tilted closest to the Sun. This is the summer **solstice**, the longest day of the year, the one that has the most sunlight. Following the summer solstice, the days begin to get shorter. Six months later, on December 21 or 22, the Northern Hemisphere is angled farthest away from the Sun. This is the winter solstice, the day when Earth get the least amount of sunlight all year. After the winter solstice occurs, the days begin to get longer again.

The farther energy travels, the weaker it becomes, especially when it passes through Earth's **atmosphere**.

Globes are tilted at an angle, which represents the axial tilt of Earth.

The atmosphere is filled with water vapor, dust, and other matter that soaks up some energy and reflects some away from Earth. When the Sun's energy passes through more of the atmosphere, more of the energy is filtered out. Then it reaches Earth's surface as **indirect light**. At this point, the light is darker and cooler than when it started out.

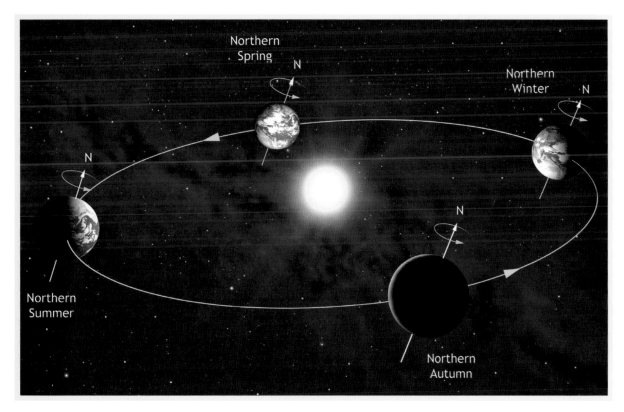

The Northern Hemisphere's ever-changing distance from the Sun gives us the seasons we are used to.

This is why we experience changing **seasons** in most parts of the United States and the rest of the Northern Hemisphere. We are used to the weather changing throughout the year. We experience a warm spring, a hot summer, a cool autumn, and a cold winter. But this familiar cycle is very different in other parts of the world. In some places, it does not even happen at all.

The area of Earth near the **equator** changes its position very little in relation to the Sun. The equator is an invisible line that wraps around the center of Earth. It is the point on Earth's surface that is always closest to the Sun, so it is exposed to the most **direct light**. The areas near the equator are the hottest places on Earth, and the ones where there is the least seasonal change.

There are only two days every year, halfway between the solstices, when day and

Each of Earth's hemispheres experiences summer when it is closest to the Sun and winter when it is farthest from the Sun.

18

night are the same length in both hemispheres. These are the **equinoxes** (from a Latin word meaning "equal night")—the days when the Sun's light strikes the equator straight on. When this happens, on March 20 or 21 and again on September 22 or 23, day and night are both twelve hours long.

At the North Pole and the South Pole, the seasons do not work the way most of us are used to. In the Arctic, in the far north, Earth's surface is angled away from the Sun for much of the winter months, and the sky is permanently dark. Then, when summer comes, there is a long period when the Sun never sets. Exactly the opposite is true at the South Pole, in Antarctica. Everything, including the seasons, is reversed in the Southern Hemisphere, because that part of the planet is always facing in the direction opposite to the Northern Hemisphere. This is why it is summer in Australia when it is winter in North America.

The planet Neptune is so far away from the Sun's heat that it is one of the coldest in the Solar System.

The Sun at Work

The Sun is at the center of all our lives. The Sun's energy warms the planet's surface and makes it possible for human beings and other life forms to survive. Planets that are far away from the Sun—such as Neptune—are almost certainly too cold to support life of any kind.

As the Sun sets, Earth grows cooler. When the Sun rises again, the planet grows warmer again. This never-ending cycle of warming and cooling sets powerful natural forces in

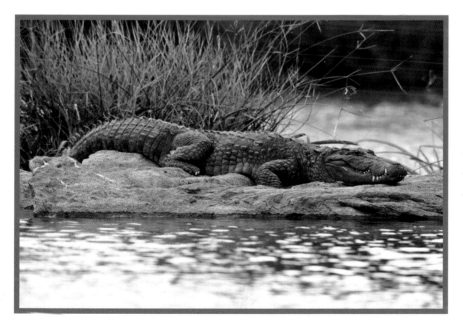

Cold-blooded animals, like this crocodile, cannot survive without the Sun's heat to warm their bodies.

motion, from the winds that blow to the clouds that pour rain from the sky.

The Sun provides nearly all of the energy used on Earth, sometimes in surprising ways. One of the most important ways is **photosynthesis**—the process by which plants take sunlight and convert it into the oxygen we breathe. Even the

The solar panels on the roof of this house store the sun's energy and turn it into electricity.

oil and natural gas we use to power our cars and to heat our homes come from the Sun. These **fossil fuels** are the remains of prehistoric plants that stored the Sun's energy, then rotted away and were buried underground for millions of years.

The Sun produces so much energy that, if the atmosphere did not filter some of it out, it could damage or even destroy much of the life on Earth. Some forms of energy from the Sun, such as **ultraviolet light**, can be extremely harmful to

The particles of matter in Earth's atmosphere filter out much of the Sun's energy, and give us the beautiful colors of sunset.

human beings. It can cause severe burns and serious diseases such as skin cancer. The water, dust, and other matter in the atmosphere absorbs much of this light and make life much safer on Earth.

The filtering effect of the atmosphere is responsible not only for protecting us from the Sun's harmful energy, but also for the displays of color we see at sunset. The matter in the

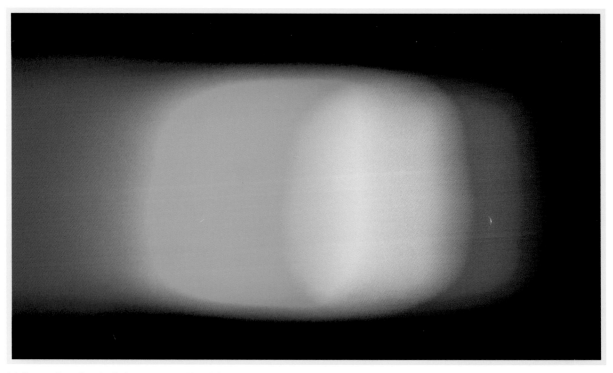

When the Sun's light enters Earth's atmosphere, it is broken up into the different parts of the color spectrum, as shown here.

atmosphere both absorbs light and breaks it up. Light gets broken into different **wavelengths**, or parts of the **color spectrum**, in a process called **scattering**. Colors that have shorter wavelengths, such as blue, are scattered the most. This is why the sky usually looks blue in the daytime. In the evening, when a point on Earth's surface is moving farther away from the Sun, the blue light gets scattered even more. This allows colors with longer wavelengths, such as reds, oranges, and yellows, to pass through. This gives a sunset its reddish glow.

Activity

You can create the cycle of night and day, sunset and sunrise, right at home.

What You Will Need
* a globe
* a flashlight or lamp
* masking tape or colored electrical tape
* a room that can be dark

What To Do
Place the globe on a flat surface in the room, such as a table or desk or the floor. Note where the North Pole, the South Pole, and the equator are located. Find where you live on the globe and mark the spot with a piece of the tape.

   If the globe is not already tilted, place it at a slight angle. Now place the flashlight or lamp some distance away from the globe and turn it on. If you are using a flashlight, you may need someone to hold it for you. Remember that flashlights and lamps get very hot. Do not touch the bulb. Make the room dark by turning out the lights or closing the curtains.

Now, looking down from above the North Pole, rotate the globe slowly in a counterclockwise direction. Focus your attention on the place where you live. You will see that the "sunlight" passes over the globe. The Sun will set on your hometown and then, eventually, rise again.

 Glossary

astronomer—Scientists who study space.

atmosphere—The air surrounding Earth, and all the matter contained in it.

axial tilt—The constant angle of Earth's axis in relation to the Sun.

axis—An invisible line around which a body (such as Earth) rotates.

color spectrum—The entire range of colors.

direct light—Light that is relatively strong because it passes through little of the atmosphere before reaching Earth's surface.

energy—The ability to do work or produce heat.

equator—An invisible horizontal line running around the center of Earth.

equinoxes—The two days every year when day and night are the same length.

fossil fuels—A fuel (such as coal, oil, or natural gas) that is formed in the ground from the remains of plants or animals.

gravity—A force that causes one body in space to attract another.

indirect light—Light that is relatively weak because it passes through a large amount of the atmosphere before reaching Earth's surface.

light—A visible form of energy.

light-year—The distance that light travels in one year—5.9 trillion miles (9.5 trillion km)

mass—The amount of matter that an object contains.

moon—Bodies that orbit a planet.

Northern Hemisphere—The half of Earth north of the equator.

orbit—The path that a body in space follows as it revolves around another body.

photosynthesis—The process by which plants convert light into oxygen.

planet—A large body that orbits a star.

rotate—Spinning on an axis.

scattering—The process by which the atmosphere breaks light into different wavelengths.

seasons—The natural divisions (spring, summer, autumn, and winter) of the year.

solar system—A system of planets and other bodies that orbit a single star.

solstice—The day of the year that has either the longest or the shortest period of sunlight.

star—A huge ball of burning gases spinning in space.

Sun—A star that is the center of a solar system.

ultraviolet light—A type of light that is invisible to the human eye.

universe—All the matter and energy in existence.

wavelength—The size of a wave of energy (such as light).

# Find Out More

BOOKS

Haddox-Baldwin, Carol, et. al. *Earth, Moon, and Sun* (Delta Science Readers). Nashua, NH: Delta Education, 2006.

Hill, Steele and Michael Carlowicz. *The Sun*. New York: Abrams, 2006.

Mara, Wil. *Why Is the Sky Blue?* (Tell Me Why, Tell Me How). Tarrytown, NY: Marshall Cavendish Benchmark, 2007.

WEB SITES

Facts about the Sun and Sundials
www.diduknow.info/Sun

Kids Astronomy
www.kidsastronomy.com

Solar Views
www.solarviews.com/eng/homepage.htm

Index

Page numbers in **boldface** are illustrations.